The Northwest Territories

Heather Kissock

WEIGL EDUCATIONAL PUBLISHERS

Published by Weigl Educational Publishers Limited
6325 10 Street SE
Calgary, Alberta, Canada
T2H 2Z9
Web site: www.weigl.com

We acknowledge the financial support of the Government of Canada through the Book Publishing
Industry Development Program (BPIDP) for our publishing activities.

National Library of Canada Cataloguing in Publication Data
Kissock, Heather
  The Northwest Territories / Heather Kissock.
  (Canadian sites and symbols)
  Includes index.
  ISBN 1-55388-028-5
  1. Provincial emblems--Northwest Territories--Juvenile literature.
2. Heraldry--Northwest Territories--Juvenile literature. I. Title. II. Series.
CR213.N7K57 2003   j929.6'09719'2   C2003-910535-0

Printed in the United States of America
1 2 3 4 5 6 7 8 9 0   07 06 05 04 03

Project Coordinator: Donald Wells
Design: Janine Vangool
Layout: Virginia Boulay
Copy Editor: Tina Schwartzenberger
Photo Researcher: Ellen Bryan

Photograph Credits
Every reasonable effort has been made to trace ownership and to obtain permission to reprint
copyright material. The publishers would be pleased to have any errors or omissions brought to
their attention so that they may be corrected in subsequent printings.

Cover: traditional campsite (**Tessa Macintosh**); **Barrett & MacKay**: page 15; **CORBIS/MAGMA**: page 17T;
Corel Corporation: pages 3T, 3M, 3B, 7T, 13T, 20, 21, 23; **Lyn Hancock**: pages 4, 5, 11, 13B, 14, 22; **Ray
Joubert**: page 10; **Tessa Macintosh**: pages 7B, 18; **National Archives of Canada**: page 6 (PA-14384);
Photos.com: pages 9, 17B; **Duane S. Radford/Lone Pine Photo**: page 12; **Territorial Government of
the Northwest Territories**: pages 1, 8, 19; **Travel Montana/S. Shimek**: page 16.

Contents

Introduction

Canada is a large country. The ten Canadian provinces and three territories cover a vast amount of land. From one province or territory to another, the people, lifestyles, land, and animals are quite different. Each province and territory has its own **identity**. The provinces and territories use **symbols** to represent this identity. This book looks at the symbols that represent the Northwest Territories.

Only lichens, dwarfed shrubs, and mosses can grow In the northern parts of the Northwest Territories.

Yukon Territory

Nunavut

Northwest Territories

British Columbia

Alberta

Manitoba

Saskatchewan

The Northwest Territories is one of Canada's three territories. It lies in the northwest part of Canada. When people think about the Northwest Territories, they usually imagine the ice, snow, and mountains of the Far North. This territory also has thick forests, sparkling lakes, and plenty of wildlife. All of the Northwest Territories' official symbols are connected to its natural **heritage**.

Ontario

Quebec

Newfoundland and Labrador

Prince Edward Island

New Brunswick

Nova Scotia

0	Kilometres	500
0	Miles	310.69

N

Fun Facts

Yellowknife is the capital of the Northwest Territories. It is also the only city in the territory.

The Northwest Territories covers 1.17 million square kilometres (451,740 square miles)—almost 13 percent of Canada.

More than 40,000 people live in the Northwest Territories.

What's in a Name?

The Northwest Territories was named for its location in northwestern Canada. In 1870, the Canadian government purchased a large amount of land from Great Britain and the Hudson's Bay Company. The land extended far north and west of central Canada. The government called the whole region the Northwest Territories. The territory was once much larger than it is today. Large parts of the Northwest Territories have become provinces and other territories.

The Hudson's Bay Company is one of the world's oldest companies. It had been in business for 200 years when Canada became a country in 1867.

The Northwest Territories is nicknamed the "Land of the Midnight Sun" because the Sun shines at midnight during the summer. In some parts of the territory, the summer Sun does not set for 24 hours on the summer solstice, the longest day of the year. The Northwest Territories is also known as the "Land of the Long Night" because the winter nights are quite long. In some parts of the territory, the Sun does not rise for 24 hours on the winter solstice, the shortest day of the year.

The Sun seldom sets in Arctic communities during the summer. In order to sleep, many people in the Northwest Territories cover their windows with blankets or tin foil to block the sunlight.

At one time, the Northwest Territories included all of Alberta, Nunavut, Saskatchewan, and the Yukon. It also included most of Manitoba, Ontario, and Quebec.

The Northern Lights are moving ribbons of red or green light. These lights are seen most often in the northern night sky. Northern lights have been described as shimmering midnight rainbows.

Coat of Arms Closeup

A coat of arms is a special design that stands for a group or a region. Every Canadian province and territory has its own coat of arms. The Northwest Territories' coat of arms was approved by Queen Elizabeth II on February 7, 1957. The coat of arms honours the territory's Arctic heritage. Each part of the design stands for a certain aspect of life in the North.

Fun Facts

The Northwest Territories' coat of arms is in the centre of the territory's official seal.

Both the crest and shield of the Northwest Territories are based on the coat of arms design.

Features

The top of the coat of arms shows two **narwhals** guarding a compass rose. The compass rose symbolizes the magnetic North Pole.

white fox

The wavy blue line symbolizes the Northwest Passage, a waterway connecting the Atlantic and Pacific Oceans.

The white background represents the territory's polar ice.

The white fox's head represents the fur of the many animals found in the area.

The red represents the tundra that makes up the northern parts of the territory.

A black diagonal line separates the green from the red. It symbolizes the tree line, where trees stop growing and the **tundra** begins.

The green on the lower part of the shield stands for the forests found in the southern parts of the territory.

Flying the Flag

When the time came to create a flag for the Northwest Territories, the territorial government decided to hold a contest. People across Canada were invited to design a flag and enter it in the contest. Robert Bessant from Manitoba designed the winning flag. The Northwest Territories made his design the official flag in 1969.

The territorial shield sits in the middle of the flag. The shield lies on a white background representing the ice and snow of the North. On each side of the white is a band of blue. The blue represents the Northwest Territories' many lakes and rivers. Great Bear Lake is the eighth largest lake in the world, and Great Slave Lake is the tenth largest lake in the world. These are the largest lakes in the Northwest Territories.

Fun Facts

Canada's longest river, the MacKenzie, flows through the Northwest Territories.

The highest mountain in the territory with a name is Mount Sir James MacBrien. It is 2,700 metres (8,858 feet) high.

The MacKenzie River is an important transportation route in the Northwest Territories. Ships can only sail up the MacKenzie River for 4 months of the year. The river is frozen for the rest of the year.

Arctic Graylings and Gyrfalcons

The Northwest Territories is home to Arctic foxes, caribou, grizzly bears, muskox, and polar bears. Narwhals, seals, walruses, and whales swim in the Arctic Ocean. The Northwest Territories' official fish is the Arctic grayling, a rare fish that swims in the territory's freshwater streams. The Arctic grayling has a dark body, grey sides, and shiny red and purple spots on its sail-shaped **dorsal** fin. The Arctic grayling lives in the harshest **environments**.

Arctic graylings can live through long Arctic winters when rivers are frozen and there is little oxygen in the water.

The official bird of the Northwest Territories is the gyrfalcon. It is one of the few birds that spends all year in the territory. Most other birds fly south for the winter. The gyrfalcon is the largest type of falcon. It is an excellent hunter and flyer. Its colour ranges from white to grey to deep brown.

Fun Facts

Polar bears often roam the streets of northern communities in search of food.

The license plates of the Northwest Territories are shaped like a polar bear. A schoolboy from Yellowknife designed the plates in 1970.

In the summer, more than 200 types of birds can be found in the Northwest Territories.

The gyrfalcon's diet consists mostly of ptarmigan, a small Arctic bird. These animals are closely connected. If there are no ptarmigans to eat, there will be fewer gyrfalcons as well.

Northern Plants

It is difficult for plants to survive in the Far North. The weather is very cold for much of the year. In the summer, wildflowers bloom all over the Northwest Territories. The territory's official flower is the mountain avens, a member of the rose family. It is a small shrub that grows close to the ground. The mountain avens has a short stem with narrow leaves and a single white and yellow flower. It grows on high, barren, rocky ground. The mountain avens is the most common flower in the Arctic region.

In the past, mountain avens were important to the Inuit. When the top of the mountain avens began to twist, the Inuit knew it was time to move inland to hunt caribou.

The tamarack is the official tree of the Northwest Territories. It has flat, soft needles that are bright green in colour. Although the tamarack looks like an evergreen tree, it has one important difference. While an evergreen tree keeps its needles all year, a tamarack sheds its needles every autumn. The needles turn a golden colour before they fall. The tamarack is the only **conifer** that sheds its needles in this way.

Tamarack trees provide food for many animals. Deer nibble on the bark, squirrels store the cones for winter, and porcupines eat the sap.

Fun Facts

The Inuit used large bundles of cottongrass to line infants' trousers—perhaps the world's first disposable diapers.

Tamarack sap can be eaten as a sweet treat. The bark can be used to treat burns.

Arctic plants are covered in hair. These hairs keep plants from freezing in the cold temperatures and bitter winds of the Arctic. The hairs radiate heat back toward the plant and trap a thin layer of warm air against the plant.

Emblems of the Earth

The Northwest Territories is known for its rocky **terrain**. This terrain contains many different minerals and gems. The mining of minerals and gems contributed $1.3 billion to the Northwest Territories' economy in 2002. Gold is the official mineral of the Northwest Territories. It represents the territory's wealth and bright future. Gold has helped to build the territory's economy. In 1935, gold was discovered at the Con-Rycon mine near Yellowknife. Gold is still being recovered from the Con-Rycon mine.

Many people moved to the Northwest Territories to work in the gold industry. Today, most of the territory's residents work for the federal, territorial, and municipal governments.

The diamond is the official gemstone of the Northwest Territories. Diamonds were discovered in the territory in 1991. Like gold, they have helped to build the territory's economy. The Northwest Territories is home to Canada's first diamond mine, the Ekati Diamond Mine. It has become one of the world's largest diamond mines.

Diamonds from the Ekati diamond mine in the Northwest Territories are some of the world's most expensive diamonds. The mine produces $1.7 million worth of diamonds every day.

Fun Facts

Oil and natural gas are found in many parts of the Northwest Territories.

The Northwest Territories is rich in minerals and metals. Most of these minerals and metals are found in the parts of the Northwest Territories that lie on the **Canadian Shield.**

A Symbolic Staff

The Northwest Territories has an official mace. A mace is an ornamental stick that is carried as a symbol of authority. It represents the power of the territory's government. The sergeant at arms carries the mace into parliament at the beginning of each daily session. It stays there as long as the Speaker of the House is in the chair. The Northwest Territories' mace celebrates the territory's Arctic heritage. It has many interesting features.

The round shape of the Legislative Chamber represents the consensus form of government used in the Northwest Territories and the cultural traditions of the Inuit people.

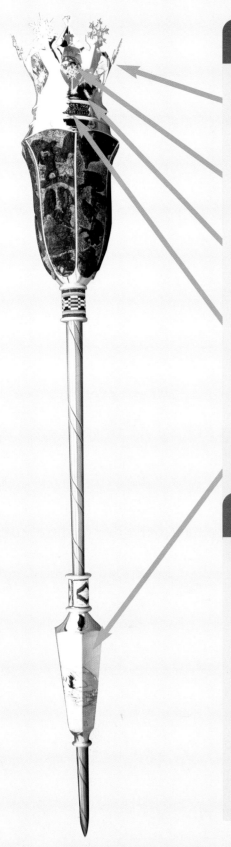

Features

The crown of snowflakes represents the territory's link to the British **monarchy**.

A golden ball inside the crown symbolizes the midnight Sun, the circle of life, and the world.

A northern diamond sits on top of the mace's crosspiece.

Inside a silver band, the words "One Land, Many Voices" are engraved in the territory's ten languages.

Below the shaft is a six-sided silver foot. The territory's entire landscape is carved on this foot.

Fun Facts

Native Peoples make up about half the Northwest Territories' population. The three main groups of Native Peoples are the Dene, Inuit, and Métis.

Tiny pebbles inside the territorial mace make a ringing sound whenever the mace moves. This sound represents the voices of the people who live in the Northwest Territories.

Special Places

Every province and territory has at least one special place that represents its heritage. This place can be a historic fort, a monument, or a park. The Northwest Territories has two very important parks—Nahanni National Park and Wood Buffalo National Park. These parks are symbols of the North's untouched wilderness. They represent the territory's natural heritage. Nahanni National Park is famous for its beautiful scenery. It has powerful rivers and waterfalls, as well as deep canyons, tall mountains, and alpine tundra.

There are waterfalls, rapids, and hot springs along the South Nahanni river. The river flows through the Nahanni National Park. It was named a Canadian Heritage River in 1987.

Wood Buffalo National Park covers 44,807 square kilometres (17,300 square miles). Not only is it Canada's largest national park, it is one of the largest parks in the world. Like Nahanni National Park, Wood Buffalo National Park is known for its beautiful scenery. Many **endangered species** live in this park. It is home to one of the world's largest free-roaming buffalo herds and the last natural nesting area of the whooping crane. Nahanni National Park and Wood Buffalo National Park are both World Heritage Sites.

In 1925, 7,000 plains buffalo were moved to Wood Buffalo National Park. They bred with the wood buffalo and created a mixed species.

Fun Facts

Wood Buffalo National Park was established in 1922 to protect the habitat of a small herd of wood buffalo. The buffalo population had dropped from about 40 million in 1830 to less than 1,000 by 1900.

The only way to get to Nahanni National Park is by aircraft.

Virginia Falls is a 90-metre (295-feet) waterfall in Nahanni National Park. This waterfall is almost twice as high as Niagara Falls, which is 55 metres (180 feet) high.

Quiz

Based on what you have read, see if you can answer the following questions:

1. What is the capital of the Northwest Territories?

2. What is the name of Canada's largest national park?

3. What animals appear on the Northwest Territories' coat of arms?

4. What makes a tamarack tree different from other evergreen trees?

Sled dog racing is a popular sport in the Northwest Territories. The Canadian Championship Dog Derby is held every spring near Yellowknife.

5. What is the shape of the Northwest Territories' license plate?

6. What is the official gemstone of the Northwest Territories?

7. Does the gyrfalcon spend the winter months in the Northwest Territories?

8. What is the Northwest Territories' nickname?

The entire MacKenzie River system is more than 4,241 kilometres (2,635 miles) long. The river attracts many summer visitors, who camp and canoe from Great Slave Lake to the Arctic Ocean.

Answers

8. The Land of the Midnight Sun or the Land of the Long Night

7. Yes

6. The diamond

5. The license plate is shaped like a polar bear.

4. The tamarack tree sheds its needles every autumn.

3. Narwhal, fox

2. Wood Buffalo National Park

1. Yellowknife

Glossary

Canadian Shield: an area of ancient rock that covers part of Canada

conifer: a tree that has cones and needles

dorsal: located on the back

endangered species: a group of animals that are in danger of becoming extinct

environments: areas in which something lives

heritage: something handed down from earlier generations

identity: the qualities that make one person or thing different from all others

monarchy: a nation or state ruled by a king or queen

narwhals: small Arctic whales

symbols: things that stand for something else

terrain: ground or land

tundra: a large, treeless plain in the Arctic

Index

The Arctic Tern's Journey

Benjamin Tunby

Lerner Publications • Minneapolis

Lerner Publications Company
A division of Lerner Publishing Group, Inc.
241 First Avenue North
Minneapolis, MN 55401 USA

For reading levels and more information, look up this title at www.lernerbooks.com.

Library of Congress Cataloging-in-Publication Data

Names: Tunby, Benjamin.
Title: The Arctic tern's journey / Benjamin Tunby.
Description: Minneapolis : Lerner Publications, [2018] | Series: Lightning bolt books. Amazing migrators | Audience: Age 6-9. | Audience: K to grade 3. | Includes bibliographical references and index.
Identifiers: LCCN 2017014443 (print) | LCCN 2017012900 (ebook) | ISBN 9781512497809 (eb pdf) | ISBN 9781512486346 (lb : alk. paper)
Subjects: LCSH: Arctic tern—Juvenile literature. | Arctic tern—Migration—Juvenile literature. | Terns—Juvenile literature.
Classification: LCC QL696.C46 (print) | LCC QL696.C46 T86 2018 (ebook) | DDC 598.3/38—dc23

LC record available at https://lccn.loc.gov/2017014443

Manufactured in the United States of America
1-43458-33198-5/23/2017

Table of Contents

Meet the Arctic Tern

An arctic tern glides through the air. Arctic terns are migrators. They move from one area to another at different times of the year.

The arctic tern's wings stretch 2.5 feet (0.8 m) from tip to tip!

An arctic tern is light gray with a large black spot on its head. Its beak and legs are red.

The tern's narrow wings and short legs help it fly long distances. Arctic terns have the longest migration of any known animal.

Most birds' bones are hollow. This makes them lighter and helps them fly more easily.

In April, artic terns start their journey. They fly north for thousands of miles to the Arctic.

Arctic terns rest on floating ice to get ready for their long journey.

An Arctic Tern Hatches

Arctic terns mate near the Arctic between May and July. They live on islands, rocky beaches, and tundra.

Females lay one to three light, spotted eggs. The chicks hatch after about twenty-four days. They take their first flight in three to four weeks.

Arctic terns make their nests on the ground.

Arctic tern parents protect and feed their chicks. Young terns are ready to migrate to the Antarctic after about three months.

An Arctic Tern Migrates

Arctic terns can't find enough fish and insects when it gets cold in the Arctic. They will migrate to the Antarctic to find more food.

Arctic terns eat fish and insects. They fly over the water and dive to catch food.

Arctic terns fly south
for about three months
during their migration.
They travel a winding
path over the sea. The
terns feed along the way.

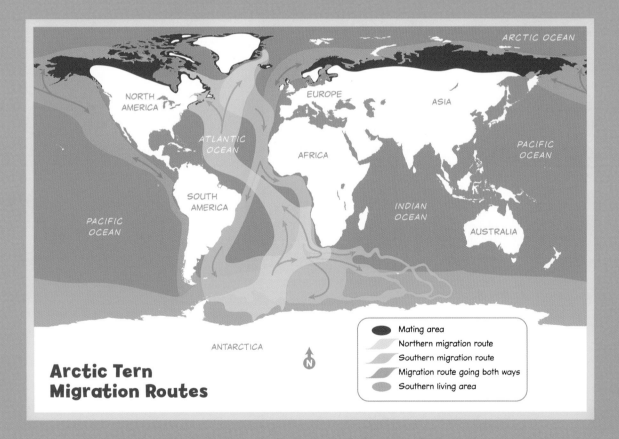

Arctic Tern Migration Routes

- Mating area
- Northern migration route
- Southern migration route
- Migration route going both ways
- Southern living area

Arctic terns will migrate back to the Arctic in February or March. They go there to mate again. That trip takes only about forty days.

The trip north is much faster than the migration south. Winds push arctic terns along as they return to the Arctic.

Young arctic terns stay in Antarctica while the adults fly back. These terns will migrate back to the Arctic to mate in a couple of years.

Arctic terns can mate when they are about four years old.

Scientists think arctic terns fly about 45,000 miles (72,000 km) a year during migration. In their lifetime, terns travel the same number of miles you would travel to get to the moon and back three times!

Arctic Terns in Danger

Kee-errr! An arctic tern calls in alarm. A fox is near the tern's nest. The parents dive at the fox. This scares the fox away.

Arctic terns protect themselves and their young. They will fight off anything that gets too close!

Foxes and other predators are dangerous for arctic terns. But an even bigger danger is people. People are hurting Earth by making it warmer.

Many people enjoy looking at arctic terns. But people's actions sometimes harm these birds.

Arctic terns live in the Arctic and Antarctic. These areas are affected by Earth's warming. The changing temperatures change terns' habitat and food supply. So arctic terns might need to find a new place to live.

Wasting energy is one thing that can make Earth warmer. But you can help stop waste! Using less energy can help. For example, turn the lights off when you leave a room. We can work together to protect the terns' habitat.

We can all help arctic terns by doing what's good for Earth!

Fun Facts

- Arctic terns are well-known birds. Many countries honor them. The bird has been on postage stamps in Canada, Finland, Iceland, and other countries.

- Arctic terns grow new feathers in winter. They rarely fly then. They rest on floating ice.

- Antarctica has nearly twenty-four hours of sunlight each day from December through February. The Arctic also has long, sunny days from June through August. So arctic terns may see the most sunlight of any animal.

More Amazing Migrators

- The sooty shearwater travels almost as far as the arctic tern. It flies up to 40,000 miles (64,400 km) a year.

- Straw-colored fruit bats live throughout Africa. They can migrate in groups of millions.

- Not all birds fly. Emperor penguins migrate by walking.

Glossary

Antarctic: an area near the South Pole. The region is in the continent of Antarctica.

Arctic: an area near the North Pole

habitat: a place where animals live

mate: when a male and a female come together to produce young

migrator: an animal that moves from one area to another at different times of the year

predator: an animal that eats other animals

tundra: a cold, treeless area near the Arctic

Further Reading

Boothroyd, Jennifer. *Let's Visit the Tundra*. Minneapolis: Lerner Publications, 2017.

Easy Science for Kids: Terns and Their Lifestyle
http://easyscienceforkids.com/all-about-terns

Enchanted Learning: Arctic Tern
http://www.enchantedlearning.com/subjects/birds/printouts/Arcticternprintout.shtml

Hirsch, Rebecca E. *Arctic Tern Migration*. Mankato, MN: Child's World, 2012.

Hirsch, Rebecca E. *Thousand-Mile Fliers and Other Amazing Migrators*. Minneapolis: Lerner Publications, 2017.

Index

Photo Acknowledgments

The images in this book are used with the permission of: © iStockphoto.com/abzerit, p. 2;
© iStockphoto.com/Bill_Dally, p. 4; © iStockphoto.com/bearacreative, p. 5; © iStockphoto.
com/TahirAbbas, pp. 6, 11; © iStockphoto.com/Pengranger, p. 7; Incredible Arctic/
Shutterstock.com, p. 8; fotoslavt/Shutterstock.com, p. 9; Roger Hall/Shutterstock.com,
p. 10; © Laura Westlund/Independent Picture Service, p. 12; © David Woodfall/NPL/Minden
Pictures, p. 13; Curioso/Shutterstock.com, p. 14; Alexander Erdbeer/Shutterstock.com, p. 15;
David Tipling Photo Library/Alamy Stock Photo, p. 16; blickwinkel/Alamy Stock Photo, p. 17;
ginger_polina_bublik/Shutterstock.com, p. 18; Dmytro Vietrov/Shutterstock.com, p. 19;
© iStockphoto.com/ChrisPole, p. 20; © iStockphoto.com/Gannet77, p. 22.

Front cover: Attila JANDI/Shutterstock.com, front cover.

Main body text set in Billy Infant regular 28/36. Typeface provided by SparkType.